A JOURNAL
of THANKSGIVING

Record Three Years of Gratitude in a Sentence a Day

Compiled and edited by Nicole M. Roccas

ANCIENT FAITH PUBLISHING ☩ CHESTERTON, INDIANA

A Journal of Thanksgiving: Record Three Years of Gratitude in a Sentence a Day
Copyright ©2020 Nicole M. Roccas

All rights reserved. No part of this publication may be reproduced by any means, electronic, mechanical, photocopying, recording, scanning, or otherwise, without the prior written permission of the Publisher.

Published by:
   Ancient Faith Publishing
   A Division of Ancient Faith Ministries
   P.O. Box 748
   Chesterton, IN 46304

All Old Testament quotations, unless otherwise identified, are from the Orthodox Study Bible, ©2008 by St. Athanasius Academy of Orthodox Theology (published by Thomas Nelson, Inc., Nashville, Tennessee) and are used by permission.

Quotations of individual prayers are taken from the *Ancient Faith Prayer Book* (Ancient Faith Publishing, 2014).

ISBN: 978-1-944967-67-3

Printed in the United States of America

Dear fellow travelers,

ONE EVENING a handful of years ago, deep in the throes of a spiritual desert, I found a notebook and decided to write down one thing I was grateful to God for arising from that day. It was the beginning of a daily ritual I came to call "thanks-writing"—giving thanks through brief, one- or two-sentence recollections each day. The practice has become a way to cultivate gratitude toward God for all He has given me.

The offering of thanks stands at the heart of historical Christian spirituality and doxology. Even the Eucharist—the pinnacle of Christian fellowship and liturgy—derives from the Greek word *eucharistía*, "thanksgiving." Our worship, indeed our entire lives, is intended to be and become a continuous thank offering of ourselves back to our Father and Creator, who Himself has granted us all good things.

In gathering the quotes for this journal, I have been deeply challenged by the distinctiveness of Christian understandings of thanksgiving. Scripture and other writings of our tradition are unanimous (and insistent) that we give thanks for all things and at all times. What a departure this is from the call to gratitude we hear from pop culture and psychology, which so often instructs us to "focus on the positive" as a way to lessen the anxiety or dissatisfaction we feel toward whatever we have deemed in our lives to be "negative." To give thanks for all things is a discipline, an ascesis—it involves intentionally recognizing the facets of our existence that are painful, frustrating, shameful, burdensome, or grievous so that we may learn to give thanks for them, since "all things are ordained by the Lord's love" (St. Basil, Letter 101). It also requires we become aware of destructive tendencies like greed, pride, or mindless consumption, which are impediments to thanksgiving.

And so, throughout the pages of this journal we are enjoined to offer up thanks not only for moments of prosperity, abundance, beauty, or ease, but also for scarcity, sickness, bedrest, shipwrecks, old age, sadness, death, maltreatment, the recognition of our weaknesses, and a great many other perils that assault our lives yet have much to teach us by way of endurance, self-awareness, and compassion. Indeed, St. John Chrysostom at various times in his sermons goes so far as to assert that "it is our duty to give thanks even for hell itself" (see Homily 19 on Ephesians).

In learning to give thanks in this fashion, it's perhaps a comfort that the Bible does not command us to be thankful so much as to give thanks. Thanksgiving is first and foremost an action and a choice, not a feeling we must conjure up. And this act is inherently relational; it immediately ties us into the constellation of blessings afforded us and those around us by a loving God.

After recommending "thanks-writing" in my first book, *Time and Despondency*, as a way to combat spiritual apathy, I have encountered others who wanted to adopt the practice for themselves. With this journal, we can embark on that path together. Each day of the year begins with a quotation from Scripture, the early Fathers, or another source from Christian tradition to remind us of both the beauty and significance and the difficult nature of giving thanks.

Beneath each quotation is space to briefly record an item of thanksgiving for that day—a small space for each of three consecutive years (you may fill in the number of the year in the small boxes given). These few lines are meant to be manageable for folks unaccustomed to daily journaling, an exercise in concision for those who are. If you don't know where to begin, use the phrase "Glory to You, O God, for . . ." as a sentence starter, or check the back of this book for prompts. The multi-year capacity of this journal provides an ongoing record of God's small mercies in our lives that we are prone to forget with time.

Although the pages are dated beginning with January 1, there is no need to wait to begin. Just start with the current date and work through the year, then another year, then a third.

May we learn, day by day and year by year, the joy of St. Paul's words to give thanks in all circumstances (I Thess. 5:18).

In Christ's love,

Nicole Roccas

P.S. Share in the journey on social media with the hashtag #ThanksWritingAFP

January 1

Let us be glad in the Lord and rejoice that there has dawned for us the day of ever-new redemption, of ancient preparation, of eternal bliss. For as the year rolls round, there recurs for us the commemoration of our salvation, which promised from the beginning, accomplished in the fullness of time will endure forever.

(St. Leo the Great, Sermon 22)

20 _____

20 _____

20 _____

January 2

Just as athletes win crowns by their struggles in the arena, so are Christians brought to perfection by the trial of their temptations, if only we learn to accept what the Lord sends us with patience, with all thanksgiving. All things are ordained by the Lord's love.

(St. Basil the Great, Letter 101)

20

20

20

January 3

Good and bad, life and death, poverty and wealth—
These are from the Lord.

(Wisdom of Sirach 11:14)

20

20

20

January 4

Glory to You who enlighten us with the clearness of eternal life.
(Akathist of Thanksgiving, Ikos 3)

20 ___

20 ___

20 ___

January 5

Thanks be to Him who came to His own in the guise of a stranger, because He glorified the stranger.

(St. Gregory of Nyssa, Oration 39, *On the Holy Lights*)

20

20

20

January 6

Very good are all the works of our God and Savior. And what more requisite gift is there than the element of water? For with water all things are washed and nourished, cleansed and bedewed. . . . But this is not the only thing that proves the dignity of the water. There is also that which is more honourable than all—the fact that Christ, the Maker of all, came down as the rain, and was known as a spring, and diffused Himself as a river, and was baptized in the Jordan.   (St. Hippolytus of Rome, *Discourse on the Holy Theophany*)

20___

20___

20___

January 7

From birth until now Your love has illumined my path, and has wondrously guided me towards the light of eternity; from birth until now the generous gifts of Your providence have been marvelously showered upon me. I give You thanks, with all who have come to know You, who call upon Your Name.

(Akathist of Thanksgiving, Ikos 1)

January 8

Afflictions bring us near to God, they make Him even our debtor. For when we are in prosperity, we are debtors to God: and oftentimes these things bring a judgment upon us.

(St. John Chrysostom, Homily 33 on Hebrews)

20

January 9

If anything should promote joy and gladness, let us attend to it, so that our heart may not be sad, like that of Cain; but that, like faithful and good servants of the Lord, we may hear the words, "Enter into the joy of your Lord" (Matthew 25:21).

(St. Athanasius, Letter 11)

20

20

20

January 10

In winter, I have beheld how silently in the moonlight the whole earth offers You prayer, clad in its white mantle of snow, sparkling like diamonds.

(Akathist of Thanksgiving, Ikos 12)

20

20

20

January 11

I will give thanks to You, O Lord and King,
And I will praise You as my God and Savior.
I give thanks to Your name.
For You have been my protector and helper,
And You redeemed my body from destruction.

(Wisdom of Sirach 51:1–2)

20

20

20

January 12

Even if you remain at home and are set fast in bed, do not consider your life an idle one; for you undergo more severe pains than those who are dragged, maltreated, and tortured by executioners, inasmuch as in this excessive infirmity of yours you have a perpetual executioner residing with you.

(St. John Chrysostom, Letters to Olympias)

20

20

20

January 13

Verily we are bound to give thanks, that He called us, unworthy as we were, to so great a grace that He reconciled us when we were His foes; that He vouchsafed to us the Spirit of adoption.

(St. Cyril of Jerusalem, *Catechetical Lecture 23*)

20

20

20

January 14

We thank You, O Christ our God, for You have filled us this day with Your earthly gifts.

(A Prayer After the Midday Meal)

20

20

20

January 15

Give thanks, that hereby also this cloud of sadness may be scattered from you.

(St. John Chrysostom, Homily 41 on First Corinthians)

20

20

20

January 16

Glory to You, who subdue the power of the spirits of darkness and doom to death every evil.

(Akathist of Thanksgiving, Ikos 6)

20

20

20

January 17

B less the Lord, you dews and snows,
And sing a hymn to Him,
And exalt Him beyond measure unto the ages.
(Hymn of the Three Young Men, Daniel 3:68)

20

20

20

January 18

Thanksgiving has place not for the soul and spiritual blessings alone, but also for the body, and for the good things of the body.

(St. Clement of Alexandria, *The Stromata*, Book V)

20

20

20

January 19

Glory to You for what You have revealed to us in Your mercy.
(Akathist of Thanksgiving, Ikos 7)

20

20

20

January 20

Giving thanks always for all things to God, by righteous hearing and divine reading, by true investigation, by holy oblation, by blessed prayer; lauding, hymning, blessing, praising—such a soul is never at any time separated from God.

(St. Clement of Alexandria, *The Stromata*, Book VI)

20 _Today I'm thankful to have a new president. President Joe Biden. 2021 After a disastrous 4 years of Trump!_

20

20

January 21

We must strive to bring out the gift which God has stored in our hearts, namely that sober sense of reason which in our happy days draws lines of moderation round our souls, and when troubles come recalls to our minds that we are but men, reminds us that life is full of misfortunes and that the examples of human sufferings are not a few.

(St. Basil the Great, Letter to Nectarius on the death of his son)

20

20

20

January 22

By the light of the moon nightingales sing, and the valleys and hills lie like wedding garments, white as snow.

(Akathist of Thanksgiving, Ikos 2)

20

20

20

January 23

He pours the hoarfrost like salt upon the earth,
And when it freezes, it becomes like pointed thorns.
A cold north wind blows
And ice freezes on the water,
And forms on every pool of water,
And clothes the water like armor.

(Wisdom of Sirach 43:19, 20)

20

20

20

January 24

The body is like one sent on a distant pilgrimage. It uses inns and dwellings by the way, has care of the things of the world, of the places where it halts. Yet leaving its dwelling-place and property without excessive emotion, it readily follows him that leads him away from life; by no means and on no occasion turns back; gives thanks for this sojourn, and blesses God for its departure, finally embracing the mansion that is in heaven.

(ST. CLEMENT OF ALEXANDRIA, *The Stromata*, BOOK IV)

20

20

20

January 25

Glory to You for what You reveal to me, asleep or awake.

(Akathist of Thanksgiving, Ikos 10)

20 ___

20 ___

20 ___

January 26

God wills that our prayers should not simply be requests, but thanksgivings too for what we have. For how should he ask for future things, who is not thankful for the past?

(St. John Chrysostom, Homily 14 on Philippians)

20 ___

20 ___

20 ___

January 27

Glory to You for the joy of living, moving, and being able to return Your love.

(Akathist of Thanksgiving, Ikos 5)

20

20

20

January 28

Let us give thanks then, not only that God has calmed the tempest, but that He allowed it to take place; not only that He rescued us from shipwreck, but that He permitted us to fall into such distress; and such an extreme peril to hang over us. Thus also Paul bids us "in everything give thanks."

(St. John Chrysostom, Homily 17 on the Statutes)

20

20

20

January 29

Glory to You for scattering our vain imaginations.
(Akathist of Thanksgiving, Ikos 10)

20

20

20

January 30

Afflictions draw down mercy, they draw down kindness. Prosperity on the other hand lifts up even to an insane pride, and leads also to slothfulness, and disposes a man to fancy great things concerning himself; it puffs up.

(St. John Chrysostom, Homily 33 on Hebrews)

20

20

20

January 31

I have seen how the rising sun rejoices in You, how the song of the birds is a chorus of praise to You.

(Akathist of Thanksgiving, Ikos 12)

20

20

20

February 1

Glory to You; on my knees I kiss the traces of Your unseen hand.

(Akathist of Thanksgiving, Ikos 3)

20 ___

20 ___

20 ___

February 2

He that confesses thanks to God for what he suffers will not seek revenge on him that has done him wrong, since he that takes revenge acknowledges no gratitude.

(St. John Chrysostom, Homily 8 on Colossians)

20

20

20

February 3

Glory to You for raising us from the slough of our passions through suffering.

(Akathist of Thanksgiving, Ikos 10)

20

20

20

February 4

I descended into the earth,
The bars of which are everlasting barriers;
Yet let my life ascend from corruption, O Lord, my God. . . .
With a voice of thanksgiving and praise,
I will sacrifice to You.

(Jonah's Song of Thanksgiving, Jonah 2:7, 10)

20___

20___

20___

February 5

As all the fruits of the season come in their proper time—flowers in spring, grain in summer, apples in autumn—so the fruit of winter is conversation.

(St. Basil the Great, Letter 13)

20___

20___

20___

February 6

Hardship is a great good. Narrow is the way (Matthew 7:14), and affliction thrusts us into that narrow way. He who is not pressed by affliction cannot enter.

(St. John Chrysostom, Homily 33 on Hebrews)

20

20

20

February 7

G lory to You for curing our pride of heart by humiliation.
(Akathist of Thanksgiving, Ikos 10)

20

20

20

February 8

It is not possible that a man who gives thanks for his afflictions should be overwhelmed by them. For his soul rejoices by doing what is right; immediately his conscience is bright, it exults in its own commendation; and that soul which is bright, cannot possibly be sad of countenance.

(St. John Chrysostom, Homily 8 on Colossians)

20

20

20

February 9

Across the cold chains of the centuries, I feel the warmth of Your breath, I feel Your blood pulsing in my veins. Part of time has already gone, but now You are the present.

(Akathist of Thanksgiving, Kontakion 11)

20

February 10

Set your heart right and be steadfast,
And do not strive anxiously in distress.

(Wisdom of Sirach 2:2)

20

20

20

February 11

Glory to You for what You have hidden from us in Your wisdom.
(Akathist of Thanksgiving, Ikos 7)

20

20

20

February 12

The light is sweet,
And it is good for the eyes
To behold the sun.

(Ecclesiastes 11:7)

20 _____

20 _____

20 _____

February 13

Glory to You for the signs of Your presence, for the joy of hearing Your voice and living in Your love.

(Akathist of Thanksgiving, Ikos 6)

20

20

20

February 14

We were filled with Your mercy in the morning,
And in all our days we greatly rejoiced and were glad;
Gladden us in return for the days You humbled us,
For the years we saw evil things.

(Psalm 89:14, 15)

20

20

20

February 15

Glory to You for the unquenchable fire of Your Grace.
(Akathist of Thanksgiving, Ikos 11)

20

20

20

February 16

Envy and anger will shorten your days,
And worry will bring premature old age.

(Wisdom of Sirach 30:24)

20

20

20

February 17

Glory to You for the last ray of the sun as it sets; glory to You for sleep's repose that restores us.

(Akathist of Thanksgiving, Ikos 4)

20

20

20

February 18

Nothing is holier than the tongue that in distress gives thanks to God; truly in no respect does it fall short of that of martyrs.

(St. John Chrysostom, Homily 8 on Colossians)

20

20

20

February 19

Glory to You who build Your Church, a haven of peace in a tortured world.

(Akathist of Thanksgiving, Ikos 11)

| 20 |

| 20 |

| 20 |

February 20

We must not accept anything that befalls us as grievous, even if, for the present, it intensifies our weakness. Although we may be ignorant of the reasons why each thing that happens to us is sent to us, we ought to be convinced that all that happens to us is for our good, either for the reward of our patience, or for the benefit of the soul we have received.

(St. Basil the Great, Letter 101)

20

20

20

February 21

I will give thanks to You, O Lord, with my whole heart;
I will tell of all Your wondrous things.

(Psalm 9:1)

20

20

20

February 22

Glory to You for the inventiveness of the human mind.
(Akathist of Thanksgiving, Ikos 7)

20

20

20

February 23

Just before spring arrives, one may begin to see the fresh and tender grass, the return of birds which winter had banished, and many such tokens. These are but signs of spring, not spring itself. While they may be sweet, they are indications of what is yet sweeter.

(St. Gregory of Nyssa, Letter 9)

20

20

20

February 24

Glory to You for exalting us to the highest heaven.
(Akathist of Thanksgiving, Ikos 11)

20

20

20

February 25

Let us allow our wiser thoughts to speak to us in this strain of music, that we may perhaps discover some slight alleviation of our trouble.

(St. Basil the Great, Letter to Nectarius after the death of his son)

20

20

20

February 26

How filled with sweetness are those whose thoughts dwell on You; how life-giving Your holy Word.

(Akathist of Thanksgiving, Kontakion 4)

20

20

20

February 27

Do not say, "Why were the former days better than these?" For you do not inquire wisely concerning this.

(Ecclesiastes 7:10)

20

20

20

February 28

I have heard the mysterious mutterings of the forests about You, and the winds singing Your praise as they stir the waters.

(Akathist of Thanksgiving, Ikos 12)

20

20

20

February 29

The time is not yours. At present you are strangers, and sojourners, and foreigners, and aliens; seek not honors, seek not glory, seek not authority, nor revenge; bear all things, and in this way, redeem the time; give up many things. . . . Only preserve the principal thing, I mean the faith.

(St. John Chrysostom, Homily 19 on Ephesians)

20

20

20

March 1

Glory to You for the depths of Your wisdom, the whole world a living sign of it.

(Akathist of Thanksgiving, Ikos 3)

20

20

20

March 2

Let all who hope in You be glad;
They will greatly rejoice forever,
For You will dwell in them;
And all who love Your name will boast in You.

(Psalm 5:12)

20

20

20

March 3

I have understood how the choirs of stars proclaim Your glory as they move forever in the depths of infinite space.

(Akathist of Thanksgiving, Ikos 12)

20

20

20

March 4

The Lord is near those who are brokenhearted,
And He will save the humble in spirit.

(Psalm 33:19)

20

20

20

March 5

As the wind falling upon a slackened sail would have no effect, so neither does the Spirit endure to continue in a slack soul; but there is need of much tension, of much vehemence, so that our mind may be on fire, and our conduct under all circumstances on the stretch, and braced up.

(St. John Chrysostom, Homily 34 on Hebrews)

20

20

20

March 6

The Lord is the portion of my inheritance and my cup;
You are He who restores my inheritance to me.
Portions fell to me among the best,
And my inheritance is the very finest.

(Psalm 15:5–6)

20___ _____

20___ _____

20___ _____

March 7

All nature murmurs mysteriously, breathing the depth of tenderness. Birds and beasts of the forest bear the imprint of Your love.

(Akathist of Thanksgiving, Kontakion 2)

20

20

20

March 8

Delight in the Lord,
And He will give you the requests of your heart.

(Psalm 36:4)

20

20

20

March 9

Is the day done? Give thanks to Him who has given us the sun for our daily work, and has provided for us a fire to light up the night and serve the rest of the needs of life. Let night give the other occasions of prayer. When you look up to heaven and gaze at the beauty of the stars, pray to the Lord of the visible world; pray to God the Arch-artificer of the universe, who in wisdom has made them all.

(St. Basil the Great, Homily V, *In martyrem Julittam*)

20

20

20

March 10

I will give thanks to You, O Lord my God, with my whole heart,
And I shall glorify Your name forever;
For great is Your mercy to me,
And You rescued my soul from the lowest Hades.

(Psalm 86:12, 13)

20

20

20

March 11

Let me not be deceived by the corrupting delights of this world, but rather strengthen in me the desire to attain the treasures of the world to come.

(A Prayer for the Third Hour)

20

20

20

March 12

The gentle shall inherit the earth,
And they will delight in the fullness of peace.

(Psalm 36:11)

20

20

20

March 13

Glory to You who give us light; glory to You who love us with love so deep, divine and infinite.

(Akathist of Thanksgiving, Ikos 12)

20

20

20

March 14

In the day of good things,
There is forgetfulness of bad things,
And in the day of bad things,
There is no remembrance of good things.

(Wisdom of Sirach 11:23)

20

20

20

March 15

Hope in the Lord, and work goodness;
Dwell in the land, and you shall be nurtured by its riches.

(Psalm 36:3)

20

20

20

March 16

When we do works of mercy, we must be intentional, so that thoughts for our household, cares for children, anxieties about one's wife, and fear of poverty do not slacken the sail of our souls. For if we stretch the sail on all sides by the hope of the things to come, it will receive the energy of the Spirit; and none of those perishable and wretched things shall fall upon it.

(St. John Chrysostom, Homily 34 on Hebrews)

20

20

20

March 17

Prayers offered after reading Scripture find the soul fresher and more vigorously stirred by love towards God.

(St. Basil the Great, Letter to St. Gregory)

20

20

20

March 18

Sorrow is better than laughter,
For by a sad countenance the heart is made better.

(Ecclesiastes 7:3)

20 _____

20 _____

20 _____

March 19

How glorious are You in the springtime, when every creature awakens to new life and joyfully sings Your praises with a thousand tongues.

(Akathist of Thanksgiving, Ikos 3)

20

20

20

March 20

The feast of the Resurrection occurs when the days are of equal length in the spring, which of itself reminds us that we shall no longer fight with evils only upon equal terms, vice grappling with virtue in indecisive strife, but that the life of light will prevail, the gloom of idolatry melting as the day waxes stronger.

(St. Gregory of Nyssa, Letter 1)

20

20

20

March 21

Now when the sun has traversed half the heaven in his course, so that night and day are of equal length in the spring, the upward return of human nature from death to life is the theme of this great and universal festival, which all those who have embraced the mystery of the Resurrection unite in celebrating.

(St. Gregory of Nyssa, Letter 1)

20___

20___

20___

March 22

There is nothing evil in learning our infirmities in endurance. Indeed doing so prevents us from forming a prideful opinion of our own nature by lifting ourselves up against God, and taking His glory to ourselves, rendering us ungrateful, thereby bringing much evil upon ourselves.

(St. Irenaeus, *Against Heresies*, Book V)

20

20

20

March 23

And now what is my patience?
Is it not the Lord?
And my support is from You.

(Psalm 38:8)

| 20 |

| 20 |

| 20 |

March 24

We do not institute days of mourning and sorrow, as some may consider these of Easter to be, but we keep the feast, being filled with joy and gladness.

(St. Athanasius, Letter ii)

20 _____

20 _____

20 _____

March 25

Today, the warm and flowery spring has shone forth from the cold winter, and the bright sun of rejoicing and happiness has dawned for us.

(St. John of Damascus, Homily on the Annunciation)

20

20

20

March 26

Gladness of the heart is the life of man,
And rejoicing by a man lengthens his life.

(Wisdom of Sirach 30:22)

20___

20___

20___

March 27

We have a law that bids us rejoice with them that rejoice, and weep with them that weep. But it often seems that it is in our power to put only one of these commands into practice. For there is a great scarcity in the world of people who rejoice, so that it is not easy to find with whom we may share our blessings, but there are plenty who are in the opposite case.

(St. Gregory of Nyssa, Letter 4)

20

20

20

March 28

We are sailing over a great and wide sea, full of many monsters and rocks and storms. . . . It is necessary then if we would sail with ease and without danger to stretch the sails, that is, to exercise our determination: for this is sufficient for us.

(St. John Chrysostom, Homily 34 on Hebrews)

20

20

20

March 29

I saw the Lord always before me;
Because He is at my right hand, that I may not be shaken.

(Psalm 15:8)

20___

20___

20___

March 30

Outside is the darkness of the whirlwind, the terror and howling of the storm; but in the heart, in the presence of Christ, there is light, peace, and silence: Alleluia!

(Akathist of Thanksgiving, Kontakion 5)

20

20

20

March 31

Glory to You, for the smile of awakening enlightenment. Glory to You, for all that is heavenly, foreshadowing eternal life.

(Akathist of Thanksgiving, Ikos 2)

20___

20___

20___

April 1

Accept whatever is brought upon you,
And in exchange for your humiliation, be patient.

(Wisdom of Sirach 2:4)

20

20

20

April 2

It is more blessed to give than to receive, because while the giver shares the poverty of the receiver, yet he remains diligent in providing by his own toil, not merely enough for his own needs, but also what he can give to one in want. In this way he is adorned with a double grace—by giving away his goods he emulates the self-denial of Christ, while also by his labor displaying the generosity of the rich.

(St. John Cassian, *Institutes*, Book X)

20

20

20

April 3

Glory to You who bless us with light, and with the host of angels and saints.

(Akathist of Thanksgiving, Ikos 12)

20

20

20

April 4

If the hope of Christians were limited only to this life, it would rightly be reckoned a bitter lot to be parted from the body. But if we who love God regard the sundering of the soul from these bodily fetters as the beginning of our real life, why should we grieve like those who have no hope?

(St. Basil the Great, Letter 101)

20

20

20

April 5

O Lord, our Lord, how wondrous is Your name in all the earth,
For Your splendor is exalted far beyond the heavens.

(Psalm 8:1)

20

20

20

April 6

We must strive after a quiet mind. As an eye cannot ascertain an object clearly if it wanders restlessly up and down and sideways—without fixing a steady gaze upon it—so the mind distracted by a thousand worldly cares is unable clearly to apprehend the truth.

(St. Basil the Great, Letter to St. Gregory)

20

20

20

April 7

Blessed are you, mother earth, in your fleeting loveliness, which wakens our yearning for happiness that will last forever, in the land where, amid beauty that grows not old, the cry rings out: Alleluia!

(Akathist of Thanksgiving, Kontakion 2)

20

20

20

April 8

In the day of what is good, live in that goodness,
But in the day of trouble, consider also
That God made one harmonious with the other,
That a man may not find out anything
That will come after him.

(Ecclesiastes 7:14)

20

20

20

April 9

It is not the natural tendency of spring to shine forth in its radiant beauty all at once. There come as preludes to spring the sunbeam gently warming earth's frozen surface, the bud half hidden beneath the clod, and breezes blowing over the earth, so that the fertilizing and generative power of the air penetrates deeply into it.

(St. Gregory of Nyssa, Letter 9)

20

20

20

April 10

This is the part of well-disposed persons: not simply to give thanks, but to do so with great abundance, more than they have learned, if possible, even with much ambition.

(St. John Chrysostom, Homily 6 on Colossians)

20 __

20 __

20 __

April 11

Life-giving and merciful Trinity, receive my thanksgiving for all Your goodness.

(Akathist of Thanksgiving, Kontakion 13)

20

20

20

April 12

Eat what is set before you like a human being,
And do not devour your food, lest you be despised.

(Wisdom of Sirach 31:16)

20

20

20

April 13

The end of matters is better than their beginning,
And a patient man is better than one haughty in spirit.

(Ecclesiastes 7:8)

20

20

20

April 14

Glory to You for each different taste of berry and fruit; glory to You for the sparkling silver of early morning dew.

(Akathist of Thanksgiving, Ikos 2)

20

20

20

April 15

What has Christ promised us? Not that we shall make the sun stand still, or the moon, nor that the sun shall retrace his steps, but what? . . . What need have I of the sun and the moon, and of these wonders, when the Lord of all Himself comes down and abides with me? I need these not.

(St. John Chrysostom, Homily 27 on Hebrews)

April 16

I will bless the Lord who caused me to understand.

(Psalm 15:7)

20	

20	

20	

April 17

Do not let a day go by without doing something good,
And do not let any of your desire for doing good escape you.

(Wisdom of Sirach 14:14)

20

20

20

April 18

Do we return thanks to our servants for waiting upon us? By no means. Yet God is thankful to us who do not serve Him, but instead do what is expedient for ourselves. Let us not presume, as though He owed us thanks, that He owes us more, but that we are discharging a debt. For all that we do is of debt.

(St. John Chrysostom, Homily 2 on Philemon)

20

20

20

April 19

The dark storm clouds of life bring no terror to those in whose hearts Your fire is burning brightly.

(Akathist of Thanksgiving, Kontakion 5)

20

20

20

April 20

R ich men turned poor and went hungry;
But those who seek the Lord shall not lack any good thing.

(Psalm 33:11)

20

20

20

April 21

May the Father of mercies and the God of all comfort, who disposes all things in wisdom for the best, visit you by His own grace, and comfort you by Himself, working in you that which is well-pleasing to Him, and may the grace of our Lord Jesus Christ come upon you, and the fellowship of the Holy Spirit, that you may have healing of all tribulation and affliction, and advance towards all good.

(St. Gregory of Nyssa, Letter 13)

20

20

20

April 22

If you have sinned, and God has pardoned your sin, receive your pardon and give thanks; but be not forgetful of the sin; not that you should fret yourself with the thought of it, but that you may school your soul not to grow wanton and relapse again into the same snares.

(St. John Chrysostom, Homily 12 on the Statutes)

20

20

20

April 23

You visited the earth and watered it;
You enriched it abundantly;
The river of God is filled with waters;
You prepared their food, for thus is Your preparation thereof.

(PSALM 64:10)

20

20

20

April 24

He made the Heaven, the earth, the sea, all things that exist, for our sake. Tell me, are not these marks of goodness?

(St. John Chrysostom, Homily 3 on Philemon)

20

20

20

April 25

Why is one day better than another,
When all the light of a day in the year is from the sun?

(Wisdom of Sirach 33:7)

20

20

20

April 26

You are the Source of Life, the Destroyer of Death.
(Akathist of Thanksgiving, Ikos 2)

20

20

20

April 27

As for me, it is good to cling to God,
To put my hope in the Lord.

(Psalm 72:28)

20

20

20

April 28

The Christian ought never to murmur about scarcity of necessities, or about toil or labor. There ought never to be any clamor, any behavior or agitation by which anger is expressed, any diversion of mind from the full assurance of the presence of God.

(St. Basil the Great, Letter 22)

20

20

20

April 29

In the wondrous blending of sounds it is Your call we hear; in the harmony of many voices, in the sublime beauty of music, in the glory of the works of great composers.

(Akathist of Thanksgiving, Kontakion 7)

20

20

20

April 30

Be perfectly assured of this: although the reasons for what is ordained by God are beyond us, what is arranged for us by Him who is wise and who loves us is to be accepted always, be it ever so grievous to endure.

(St. Basil the Great, Letter to Nectarius after the death of his son)

20

20

20

May 1

Let the peoples give thanks to You, O God;
Let all the peoples praise You.

(PSALM 66:4)

20

20

20

May 2

The Christian ought not to resent another's reputation, nor rejoice over any person's faults. He ought in Christ's love to grieve and be afflicted at his brother's faults, and rejoice over his brother's good deeds.

(St. Basil the Great, Letter 22)

20

20

20

May 3

O Lord, how lovely it is to be Your guest: breeze full of scents; mountains reaching to the skies; waters like boundless mirrors, reflecting the sun's golden rays and the scudding clouds.

(Akathist of Thanksgiving, Kontakion 2)

20

20

20

May 4

The Lord is good to those who wait for Him,
To the soul who will seek Him, the Good One.
He will wait for and quietly expect
The salvation of the Lord.

(LAMENTATIONS OF JEREMIAH 3:22, 23)

20

20

20

May 5

I thought of the days of old,
And I remembered the eternal years; and I meditated.

(Psalm 76:6)

20

20

20

May 6

Faith needs a generous and vigorous soul, one that rises above all things of sense and passes beyond the weakness of human reasoning. For it is not possible to become a believer without raising oneself above the common customs of the world.

(St. John Chrysostom, Homily 22 on Hebrews)

May 7

You have brought me into life as into an enchanted paradise.

(Akathist of Thanksgiving, Ikos 2)

| 20 |
| 20 |
| 20 |

May 8

If we give thanks with much joy, this is a great thing that is spoken of. For it is possible to give thanks only from fear, it is even possible to give thanks when in sorrow.

(St. John Chrysostom, Homily 2 on Colossians)

20

20

20

May 9

In the land of my captivity, I give thanks to Him.

(Tobit 13:8)

20

20

20

May 10

How beautiful are the likenesses of beautiful objects when they preserve in all its clearness the impress of the original beauty!
(St. Gregory of Nyssa, Letter 14)

20

20

20

May 11

Every man should eat and drink and experience the good in all his labor—this is God's gift to him.

(ECCLESIASTES 3:13)

| 20 |

| 20 |

| 20 |

May 12

Numbers would fail to express the multiplicity of parts of the human frame, which was made in no other way than by the great wisdom of God. . . . The flesh, therefore, is not destitute of participation in the constructive wisdom and power of God.

(St. Irenaeus, *Against Heresies*, Book V)

20

20

20

May 13

For what is there in heaven for me but You,
And what do I desire on earth besides You?
My heart and my flesh fail,
O God of my heart; and God is my portion forever.

(PSALM 72:25, 26)

| 20 |

| 20 |

| 20 |

May 14

Glory to You for the feast day of life; glory to You for the perfume of lilies and roses.

(Akathist of Thanksgiving, Ikos 2)

20

20

20

May 15

You I invoke, O God, in whom and from whom and through whom all things are true. . . . God, the Good and Fair, in whom and from whom and through whom all things are good and fair.

(St. Augustine, *Soliloquies*)

20

20

20

May 16

Guide my life, O calm Haven of the storm-tossed, and reveal the way in which I should walk.

(A Prayer for the Third Hour)

20

20

20

May 17

The day is Yours, and the night is Yours;
You created the light and the sun.

(Psalm 73:16)

| 20 |

| 20 |

| 20 |

May 18

Glory to You for what You speak to me in my heart.

(Akathist of Thanksgiving, Ikos 10)

| 20 |

| 20 |

| 20 |

May 19

My heart was glad,
And my tongue rejoiced exceedingly;
My flesh also shall dwell in hope.

(Psalm 15:9)

20

20

20

May 20

"Seek," Christ says, "and you shall find." For things sought after need much care, especially in regard of God. For many are the hindrances, many the things that darken, many that impede our perception.

(St. John Chrysostom, Homily 22 on Hebrews)

20

20

20

May 21

Bless the Lord, every shower and dew,
And sing a hymn to Him,
And exalt Him beyond measure unto the ages.

(Hymn of the Three Young Men, Daniel 3:64)

20

20

20

May 22

Y̲ou made all the boundaries of the earth;
Summer and winter, You formed these things.

(Psalm 73:17)

20

20

20

May 23

Even in the time of persecution our voice has not ceased to give thanks. For not even an enemy has so much power as to prevent us, who love the Lord with our whole heart, and life, and strength, from declaring His blessings and praises always and everywhere with glory.

(St. Cyprian of Carthage, Treatise 3)

20

20

20

May 24

My soul shall remember
And meditate within me.
I will fix this in my heart;
Therefore, I will endure.

(Lamentations of Jeremiah 3:20, 21)

20 ___

20 ___

20 ___

May 25

The basic needs of a man's life
Are water, fire, iron, salt, and wheat flour,
And milk, honey, the blood of the grape, olive oil, and clothing.
As all these things are good for the godly,
So they turn the evil into sinners.

(Wisdom of Sirach 39:26, 27)

20

20

20

May 26

Seeing that we have come to enjoy so great a benefit, we ought to be ever mindful of it, and continually to turn in our minds to the free gift of God, and to reflect upon what we have been delivered from, what we have obtained; and so we shall be thankful; so we shall heighten our love toward Him.

(St. John Chrysostom, Homily 2 on Colossians)

20

20

20

May 27

If the grass of the field is like this, how gloriously shall we be transfigured in the Second Coming after the Resurrection! How splendid our bodies, how spotless our souls.

(Akathist of Thanksgiving, Ikos 3)

20

20

20

May 28

Thanks be to You, my joy, my pride, my confidence, my God—thanks be to You for Your gifts; but preserve them to me. For thus will You preserve me; and those things which You have given me shall be developed and perfected, and I myself shall be with You, for from You is my being.

(St. Augustine, *Confessions*, Book 1)

20

20

20

May 29

D o not give yourself over to sorrow,
And do not distress yourself deliberately.

(Wisdom of Sirach 30:21)

| 20 |

| 20 |

| 20 |

May 30

Solitude is of the greatest use. It stills our passions and gives room for principle to excise them from the soul. For just as animals are more easily controlled when they are stroked, so lust, anger, fear, and sorrow—the soul's deadly foes—are better brought under the control of reason after being calmed by inaction and where there is no continuous stimulation.

(St. Basil the Great, Letter to Gregory)

20

20

20

May 31

Fear the Lord, you His saints,
For there is no want for those who fear Him.

(Psalm 33:10)

20

20

20

June 1

Praise be to You who bring low the pride of man. You bring from his heart a cry of penitence: Alleluia!

(Akathist of Thanksgiving, Kontakion 6)

20

20

20

June 2

Now that I am at the end of my life, I begin to live again and am compelled to learn the graceful versatility of character which is now sought after. But we are late learners . . . so that we are constantly constrained to blush at our awkwardness and inaptitude for this new study.

(St. Gregory of Nyssa, Letter 14)

20

20

20

June 3

May You not deliver to wild beasts the soul who gives thanks to You;
May You not forget the souls of Your poor to the end.

(Psalm 73:19)

20

20

20

June 4

Now we make offering to Him, not as though He stood in need of it, but rendering thanks for His gift, and thus sanctifying what has been created. For even as God does not need our possessions, so do we need to offer something to God.

(St. Irenaeus, *Against Heresies* IV)

20

20

20

June 5

From the rising of the sun to its setting,
Praise the name of the Lord.

(Psalm 112:3)

| 2 0 |

| 2 0 |

| 2 0 |

June 6

Our lives are not without Providence. So we have learned in the Gospel, for not a sparrow falls to the ground without the will of our Father (Matthew 10:29). . . . Let us accept what has befallen us; for if we resent it, we do not mend the past and we work our own ruin. Do not let us arraign the righteous judgment of God.

(St. Basil the Great, Letter to Nectarius's wife after the death of her son)

20

20

20

June 7

We have seen the sky like a chalice of deepest blue, where in the azure heights the birds are singing.

(Akathist of Thanksgiving, Ikos 2)

20

20

20

June 8

You made known to me the ways of life;
You will fill me with gladness in Your presence.

(Psalm 15:11)

| 20 |
| 20 |
| 20 |

June 9

Why do we carry on all our affairs with reference to the present life, which tomorrow we shall leave? Let us choose then that virtue which will sustain us through all eternity: wherein we shall be continually and shall enjoy the everlasting good things.

(St. John Chrysostom, Homily 16 on Hebrews)

20

20

20

June 10

Why are you so sad, O my soul? And why do you trouble me?
Hope in God, for I will give thanks to Him;
My God is the salvation of my countenance.

(Psalm 41:6)

| 20 |

| 20 |

| 20 |

June 11

The number of single trees is more noted than their beauty; yet they display tasteful arrangement in their planting, and that harmonious form of drawing—drawing, I call it, for the marvel belongs rather to the painter's art than to the gardener's. So readily does Nature fall in with the design of those who arrange these plants that it seems impossible to express in words.

(St. Gregory of Nyssa, Letter 15, on the beauty of a garden)

20

20

20

June 12

The earth is the Lord's, and its fullness,
The world and all who dwell therein.

(Psalm 23:1)

20

20

20

June 13

It is the Holy Spirit who makes us to find joy in each flower: the exquisite scent, the delicate color, the beauty of the Most High in the tiniest of things.

(Akathist of Thanksgiving, Ikos 2)

20

20

20

June 14

Who can fitly marvel at the boundless and incomprehensible wisdom of the Creator? Or who can render sufficient thanks to the Giver of so many blessings?

(St. John of Damascus, *An Exposition of the Orthodox Faith*, Book II)

20

20

20

June 15

As for me, I said in my prosperity,
"I shall not be shaken forever."

(Psalm 29:7)

| 20 | |

| 20 | |

| 20 | |

June 16

Glory to You; no loss is irreparable in You, Giver of eternal life to all.

(Akathist of Thanksgiving, Ikos 8)

20

20

20

June 17

That my glory may sing praise to You,
And not be pierced with sadness;
O Lord my God,
I shall give thanks to You forever.

(Psalm 29:13)

20

20

20

June 18

Let us give thanks then for all things, and not be overly curious. For it is not we that know the appointed time, but He, the Maker of time, and the Creator of the ages.

(St. John Chrysostom, Homily 4 on Colossians)

20

20

20

June 19

Meet every temptation with patient endurance. And by what various trials the faithful man is proved: by worldly loss, by accusations, by lies, by opposition, by calumny, by persecution! These and the like are the tests of the faithful.

(St. Basil the Great, Letter 42)

20

20

20

June 20

R ejoice greatly in the Lord, O righteous ones;
Praise is fitting for the upright.

(Psalm 32:1)

20

20

20

June 21

I see Your heavens resplendent with stars. How glorious are You, radiant with light!

(Akathist of Thanksgiving, Ikos 5)

20

20

20

June 22

Good, indeed very good, are all the works of our God and Savior—all of them that eye sees and mind perceives, all that reason interprets and hand handles, all that intellect comprehends and human nature understands. For what richer beauty can there be than that of the circle of heaven? And what form of more blooming fairness than that of earth's surface?

(St. Hippolytus of Rome, *Discourse on the Holy Theophany*)

June 23

Do you wish . . . to be cheerful, do you wish to employ the day? . . . Learn to sing psalms, and you shall see delight. For they who sing psalms are filled with the Holy Spirit.

(St. John Chrysostom, Homily 19 on Ephesians)

20

20

20

June 24

I repent for all those who are worried, who stagger under a burden of anxieties and do not know that they should cast all their troubles on You.

(Extracts from *Prayers by the Lake* by St. Nikolai Velimirovic)

20

20

20

June 25

We shall give thanks to You, O God;
We shall give thanks, and call upon Your name.
I shall describe all Your wonders.

(Psalm 74:2,3)

20

20

20

June 26

G lory to You who bring from the depth of the earth an endless variety of colors, tastes, and scents.

(Akathist of Thanksgiving, Ikos 3)

20

20

20

June 27

Glory to You, O Christ, for with how many good things have You filled us! How You have provided for our health! From how great monstrousness, from how great unreasonableness, You have set us free!

(St. John Chrysostom, Homily 6 on Colossians)

20

20

20

June 28

The heavens declare the glory of God;
The firmament shows the creation of His hands.

(Psalm 18:1)

20

20

20

June 29

There are indeed two limits of human life: the one we start from, and the one we end in. And so it was necessary that the Physician of our being should enfold us at both these extremities, and grasp not only the end, but the beginning too, in order to secure in both the raising of the sufferer.

(St. Gregory of Nyssa, Letter 17)

20

20

20

June 30

Glory to You for the pledge of our reawakening on that glorious last day, that day which has no evening.

(Akathist of Thanksgiving, Ikos 4)

20

20

20

July 1

G lory to You for the numberless creatures around us.
(Akathist of Thanksgiving, Ikos 3)

20____

20____

20____

July 2

Let us hold the faith steadfastly, and show forth strictness of life, that having in all things returned thanks to God, we may be counted worthy of the good things promised to them that love Him.

(St. John Chrysostom, Homily 5 on Colossians)

20

20

20

July 3

You give light wondrously
From the everlasting mountains.

(Psalm 75:5)

20

20

20

July 4

But always Anthony gave the Lord thanks and besought the sufferer to be patient, and to know that healing belonged neither to him nor to man at all, but only to the Lord, who does good when and to whom He will. The sufferers therefore used to receive the words of the old man as though they were a cure, learning not to be downhearted but rather to be longsuffering. And those who were healed were taught not to give thanks to Anthony but to God alone.

(St. Athanasius, *Life of St. Anthony*)

20

20

20

July 5

Mercy and truth met together;
Righteousness and peace kissed each other;
Truth arose from the earth,
And righteousness looked down from heaven.
For the Lord will give goodness,
And our land shall yield its fruit.

(Psalm 84:11–13)

20

20

20

July 6

Remember that all the assaults of dark and evil fortune contribute to the salvation of those who receive them with thankfulness, and are assuredly ambassadors of help.

(St. John of Damascus, *An Exposition of the Orthodox Faith*, Book II)

20

20

20

July 7

We have listened to the soothing murmur of the forest and the melodious music of the streams.

(Akathist of Thanksgiving, Ikos 2)

20

20

20

July 8

For what richer beauty is there than the chariot of the sun in its course? And what more graceful vessel than the lunar orb? And what masterpiece more wonderful than the compact mosaic of the stars? And what more productive than the seasonable winds? And what mirror is more spotless than the light of day?

(St. Hippolytus, *Discourse on the Holy Theophany*)

20

20

20

July 9

F or a man shall give thanks to You from his heart,
And he shall celebrate a feast to You with his whole heart.

(Psalm 75:11)

| 20 |

| 20 |

| 20 |

July 10

Thus do You, like the lightning, unexpectedly light up my heart with flashes of intense joy.

(Akathist of Thanksgiving, Ikos 6)

20

20

20

July 11

If any one does not believe that death is abolished, that Hades is trodden under foot, that the chains thereof are broken, that the tyrant is bound, let him look on the martyrs who frolic in the presence of death and take up the jubilant strain of the victory of Christ. O the marvel!

(St. Gregory the Wonder-worker, *On all the Saints*)

20

20

20

July 12

A man with a good and cheerful heart
Will pay attention to the food he eats.

(Wisdom of Sirach 30:25)

20

20

20

July 13

Truly, my God, You are just as great with or without the world.
(St. Nikolai Velimirovic, *Prayers by the Lake*)

20

20

20

July 14

How great and how close are You in the powerful track of the storm! How mighty Your right arm in the blinding flash of the lightning!

(Akathist of Thanksgiving, Kontakion 6)

20

20

20

July 15

I have seen altogether the tasks which God has given to the sons of men to be engaged in. He made everything beautiful in its time, and He indeed put eternity in their hearts in such a way that man may not find out the work God made from the beginning to the end.

(ECCLESIASTES 3:10–11)

20

20

20

July 16

There is nothing so pleasing to God, as for a man to be thankful.

(St. John Chrysostom, Homily 19 on Ephesians)

20 ___

20 ___

20 ___

July 17

When God gives good things I think we must thank Him, and not be angry with Him while He is controlling their distribution... For He always rules our lives better than we could choose for ourselves.

(St. Basil the Great, Letter to Eustathius the Philosopher)

20

20

20

July 18

Behold for yourself what He will do for you,
And give thanks to Him fully with the organ of speech.

(Tobit 13:7)

20

20

20

July 19

For though the fig tree will not bear fruit
And there be no grapes on the vines;
The labor of the olive tree fail
And the fields yield no food;
Though the sheep have no pasture
And there be no oxen in the cribs;
Yet I will glory in the Lord; I will rejoice in God my Savior.

(Habakkuk 3:17, 18)

20

20

20

July 20

And if the presence of a good man, through the respect and reverence which he inspires, always improves him with whom he associates, with much more reason does not he who always holds uninterrupted converse with God by knowledge, life, and thanksgiving, grow at every step superior to himself in all respects.

(St. Clement of Alexandria, *The Stromata*, Book VII)

20

20

20

July 21

All the earth is Your promised bride awaiting her spotless Husband.

(Akathist of Thanksgiving, Ikos 3)

20

20

20

July 22

Mercifulness opens the way to the heart of all creatures and brings joy. Mercilessness brings fog to the fore and creates a confined isolation.

(St. Nikolai Velimirovic, *Prayers by the Lake*)

20

20

20

July 23

Are we to give thanks for everything that befalls us? Yes; be it even disease, be it even destitution.

(St. John Chrysostom, Homily 19 on Ephesians)

20

20

20

July 24

I will both sleep and rest in peace,
For You alone, O Lord, cause me to dwell in hope.

(Psalm 4:9)

20

20

20

July 25

What then is our duty but to praise and give thanks to God, the King of all?

(St. Athanasius, Letter 10)

20

20

20

July 26

Everlasting King, Your will for our salvation is full of power. Your right arm controls the whole course of human life.

(Akathist of Thanksgiving, Kontakion 1)

20

20

20

July 27

Now the day is done. For all the boons of the day, and the good deeds of the day, we must give thanks. For omissions there must be confession. For sins voluntary or involuntary, or unknown, we must appease God in prayer.

(St. Basil the Great, Homily V, *In martyrem Julittam*)

20

20

20

July 28

May hatred never make a nest in my heart against those who plot evil against me, so that I may be mindful of their end and be at peace.

(St. Nikolai Velimirovic, *Prayers by the Lake*)

20

20

20

July 29

All the works of the Lord are good,
And He will supply every need in its hour.

(Wisdom of Sirach 39:33)

20

20

20

July 30

Glory to You for the prayers offered by a trembling soul.
(Akathist of Thanksgiving, Ikos 4)

20 _____

20 _____

20 _____

July 31

We give thanks to You, and to Your only-begotten Son, and to Your Holy Spirit; for all things of which we know and of which we know not, whether manifest or unseen.

(The Divine Liturgy of St. John Chrysostom)

20

20

20

August 1

Endurance, with which we can bear the temptations brought upon us, depends not so much on our own strength as on the mercy and guidance of God.

(St. John Cassian, *Conference* 3)

20

20

20

August 2

May neither anger against the strong nor contempt for the weak erupt in my heart! For all things are frailer than the morning dew.

(St. Nikolai Velimirovic, *Prayers by the Lake*)

20

20

20

August 3

All true beauty has the power to draw the soul towards You, and to make it sing in ecstasy: Alleluia!

(Akathist of Thanksgiving, Kontakion 7)

20___

20___

20___

August 4

We ought to give thanks for all things, even for those which seem to be grievous, for this is the part of the truly thankful man.

(St. John Chrysostom, Homily 14 on Philippians)

20

20

20

August 5

Praise the Lord, for a psalm is a good thing;
Let praise be sweet to our God.

(Psalm 146:2)

| 20 |

| 20 |

| 20 |

August 6

In this Transfiguration, the foremost object was to remove the offense of the Cross from the disciples' hearts, and to prevent their faith being disturbed by the humiliation of His voluntary Passion by revealing to them the excellence of His hidden dignity.

(St. Leo the Great, Sermon 51, *On the Transfiguration*)

20

20

20

August 7

We have tasted fruit of fine flavor and the sweet-scented honey.
(Akathist of Thanksgiving, Ikos 2)

20

20

20

August 8

It is altogether just and godly to give thanks for the crops which the earth has produced for man's use under the guiding hand of supreme Providence. And to show that we do this with ready mind, we must exercise not only the self-restraint of fasting, but also diligence in almsgiving, that from the ground of our heart also may spring the germ of righteousness and the fruit of love.

(St. Leo the Great, Sermon 17)

20 _____

20 _____

20 _____

August 9

No one can say, "This is worse than that,"
For all things will be well pleasing in their time.

(Wisdom of Sirach 39:34)

20 ___

20 ___

20 ___

August 10

We shall be best able to give thanks unto God, by withdrawing our souls and by thoroughly cleansing them by the means told to us.

(St. John Chrysostom, Homily 19 on Ephesians)

20

20

20

August 11

May your soul be gladdened by His mercy,
And may you not be put to shame when you praise Him!

(Wisdom of Sirach 51:29)

20

20

20

August 12

How awesome Your majesty! The voice of the Lord fills the fields; it speaks in the rustling of the trees.

(Akathist of Thanksgiving, Kontakion 6)

20

20

20

August 13

You I invoke, O God . . . towards whom faith rouses us, hope lifts us up, with whom love joins us. God, through whom we overcome the enemy, You I entreat.

(St. Augustine, *Soliloquies*)

20

20

20

August 14

I remembered God and was glad;
I complained, and my spirit became discouraged.

(Psalm 76:4)

| 20 | |

| 20 | |

| 20 | |

August 15

Thanks be to You who gave us life, and granted us the grace of a happy life, and restored us to that, when we had gone astray, through Your unspeakable condescension.

(St. John of Damascus, *An Exposition of the Orthodox Faith*, Book IV)

20

20

20

August 16

When we were sad, He consoled us; let us give thanks to Him now that we are joyful. In our agony He comforted us, and did not forsake us; therefore let us not betray ourselves in prosperity by declining into sloth.

(St. John Chrysostom, Homily 12 on the Statutes)

20

20

20

August 17

You are my maker, who summoned all things from non-being into life. Bless this day which You, in Your ineffable goodness, have given to me.

(Prayer at Daybreak by Elder Sophrony of Essex)

20

20

20

August 18

The faithful and true servants of the Lord, knowing that the Lord loves the thankful, never cease to praise Him, ever giving thanks unto the Lord. And whether the time is one of ease or of affliction, they offer up praise to God with thanksgiving, not reckoning these things of time, but worshipping the Lord, the God of times.

(St. Athanasius, Letter 3)

20

20

20

August 19

We give You thanks for all Your mercies, seen and unseen; for eternal life, for the heavenly joys of the Kingdom which is to be.

(Akathist of Thanksgiving, Kontakion 1)

20

20

20

August 20

Blessed are they that weep; blessed are they that mourn; for they themselves shall be comforted; they themselves shall laugh. But by laughter is meant not the noise that comes out through the cheeks from the boiling of the blood, but cheerfulness pure and untainted with despondency.

(St. Basil the Great, Homily IV, *On the Giving of Thanks*)

20 ___

20 ___

20 ___

August 21

Glorify the Lord and exalt Him as much as you are able,
For He will surpass even that.
And when you exalt Him, put forth all your strength;
Do not grow weary, for you cannot exalt Him enough.

(Wisdom of Sirach 43:30)

20

20

20

August 22

Glory to You at the hushed hour of nightfall; glory to You who cover the earth with peace.

(Akathist of Thanksgiving, Ikos 4)

20

20

20

August 23

You ought to be thankful, not to be puffed up. Haughtiness is the first act of ingratitude, for it denies the gift of grace.

(St. John Chrysostom, Homily 5 on Philippians)

20

20

20

August 24

Our Savior Himself was crucified for our sakes that by His death He might give us life, and train and attract us all to endurance.

(St. Basil the Great, Letter 42)

20

20

20

August 25

Bless the Lord, you fire and heat,
And sing a hymn to Him,
And exalt Him beyond measure unto the ages.
(Hymn of the Three Young Men, Daniel 3:66)

20___
___
___
___
___
___
___

20___
___
___
___
___
___
___

20___
___
___
___
___
___
___

August 26

And the form of a spiritual person's prayer is thanksgiving for the past, for the present, and for the future which is already made present through faith present.
(St. Clement of Alexandria, *The Stromata*, Book VII)

20

20

20

August 27

Glory to You for the warmth and tenderness of the world of nature.

(Akathist of Thanksgiving, Ikos 3)

20

20

20

August 28

All things utter a prayer to You, a silent hymn composed by You. You sustain everything that exists, and all things move together at Your command.
(St. Gregory the Theologian, A Prayer to the All-Transcendent God)

20

20

20

August 29

The voice of the Lord is in the thunder and the downpour. The voice of the Lord is heard above the waters. Praise be to You in the roar of mountains ablaze.

(Akathist of Thanksgiving, Kontakion 6)

| 20 |

| 20 |

| 20 |

August 30

We will say many things and not reach the end,
But the sum of our words is seen in this: "He is the all."

(Wisdom of Sirach 43:27)

20

20

20

August 31

We give thanks unto You, O King invisible, who, by Your measureless power, made all things and, in the greatness of Your mercy, brought all things from nonexistence into being.

(The Divine Liturgy of St. John Chrysostom)

20

20

20

September 1

Y ou will bless the crown of the year with Your goodness,
And Your fields will be filled with fatness.

(Psalm 64:12)

20

20

20

September 2

Let no one hope for present blessings, let no one promise himself the happiness of the world, because he is a Christian; but let him use the happiness he has, as he may, in what manner he may, when he may, as far as he may. While it is the present, let him give thanks for the consolation of God.

(St. Augustine, *Exposition on Psalm 92*)

20

20

20

September 3

The sun gives light and looks down on everything,
And its work is full of the Lord's glory.

(Wisdom of Sirach 42:16)

20

20

20

September 4

Glory and honor be to the Spirit, the Giver of Life, who covers the fields with their carpet of flowers, crowns the harvest with gold, and gives to us the joy of gazing at it with our eyes.

(Akathist of Thanksgiving, Ikos 2)

20

20

20

September 5

Do not seek things too difficult for you,
Nor examine what is beyond your strength.
(Wisdom of Sirach 3:20)

20

20

20

September 6

Behold another consolation, a medicine which heals grief, distress, and all that is painful. What is it? Prayer, thanksgiving in all things.

(St. John Chrysostom, Homily 14 on Philippians)

20

20

20

September 7

Glory to You for calling me into being; glory to You for showing me the beauty of the universe.

(Akathist of Thanksgiving, Ikos 1)

20

20

20

September 8

In the morning You shall hear my voice;
In the morning I will stand before You,
And I will watch.

(Psalm 5:4)

20

20

20

September 9

If you give thanks when you are in comfort and in affluence, in success and in prosperity, there is nothing great, nothing wonderful in that. What is required is for a man to give thanks when he is in afflictions, in anguish, in discouragements.

(St. John Chrysostom, Homily 19 on Ephesians)

20

20

20

September 10

Give thanks to the Lord on the lyre;
Sing praises to Him on a ten-stringed instrument.

(Psalm 32:2)

20

20

20

September 11

Let us pass no season without thanksgiving, but especially now, when the time is one of tribulation.

(St. Athanasius, Letter 3)

20

20

20

September 12

How near You are in the day of sickness. You visit the sick; You Yourself bend down to the sufferer's bed.

(Akathist of Thanksgiving, Kontakion 8)

20

20

20

September 13

It is a great injury to utter a superfluity of words when teaching, praying, or giving thanks. For it is not right to be sparing of our money but not sparing of our words; we ought rather to spare words than our money.

(St. John Chrysostom, Homily 6 on Titus)

20

20

20

September 14

Glory to You for the joy of dawn's awakening; glory to You for the new life each day brings.

(Akathist of Thanksgiving, Ikos 2)

20 _____

20 _____

20 _____

September 15

Have you dishonour? Look to the glory which through patience is laid up for you in heaven. Have you suffered loss? Fix your eyes on the heavenly riches, and on the treasure which you have put by for yourself through your good works. . . . Set expected joys over against present griefs, and thus you will preserve for yourself calm and quietness of soul.

(St. Basil the Great, Homily IV, *On the Giving of Thanks*)

20

20

20

September 16

I shall now remember the works of the Lord,
And by the words of the Lord
I shall describe His works that I see.

(Wisdom of Sirach 42:15)

20

20

20

September 17

The spiritual person is inseparable from the commandment and from hope, and is ever giving thanks to God.
(St. Clement of Alexandria, *The Stromata*, Book VII)

20

20

20

September 18

The Lord has become a place of refuge for me,
And my God, the helper of my hope.

(Psalm 93:22)

20

20

20

September 19

In the throes of sorrow and suffering You bring peace and unexpected consolation.

(Akathist of Thanksgiving, Kontakion 8)

| 20 |

| 20 |

| 20 |

September 20

Let us give thanks to the merciful God, and be amazed at the power, the lovingkindness, the wisdom, and the tender care which have been manifested.

(St. John Chrysostom, Homily 21 on the Statutes)

20

20

20

September 21

We are sustained very well on Your earth. It is good to be Your guest.

(Akathist of Thanksgiving, Ikos 2)

20

20

20

September 22

Let us give thanks unto God. For not only ought we not to be discouraged at present things, but even to show the greatest gratitude to Him for those to come.

(St. John Chrysostom, Homily 33 on Hebrews)

20

20

20

September 23

To Christ I press on, and to the Father and to the Holy Ghost I strive to be found true, judging myself unworthy of this world's goods. And yet not I because of the world, but the world because of me. Think of all these things in your heart; follow them with zeal.

(St. Basil the Great, Letter 42)

20

20

20

September 24

The breath of Your Holy Spirit inspires artists, poets, and scientists. The power of Your supreme knowledge makes them prophets and interpreters of Your laws, revealing the depths of Your creativity.

(Akathist of Thanksgiving, Ikos 7)

20

20

20

September 25

All things proclaim You, those endowed with reason and those bereft of it. All the expectation and pain of the world coalesce in You.

(St. Gregory the Theologian, A Prayer to the All-Transcendent God)

20

20

20

September 26

Losing sleep over wealth wastes away the body,
And anxiety about wealth removes sleep.

(Wisdom of Sirach 31:1)

20

20

20

September 27

Eternity watches me by the rays of distant stars. I am small, insignificant, but the Lord is at my side.

(Akathist of Thanksgiving, Ikos 5)

20

20

20

September 28

The Apostle allows us to weep with weepers, for this tear is made, as it were, a seed and loan to be repaid with everlasting joy.

(St. Basil the Great, Homily IV, *On the Giving of Thanks*)

20

20

20

September 29

Think about what is commanded you,
For you do not need what the Lord keeps hidden.
(Wisdom of Sirach 3:21)

20

20

20

September 30

It is our duty to give thanks even for hell itself, for the torments and punishments of the next world. For surely it is beneficial to those who attend to it, when the dread of hell is laid like a bridle on our hearts. Let us therefore give thanks not only for blessings which we see, but also for those which we see not, and for those which we receive against our will. For many are the blessings He bestows upon us, without our desire, without our knowledge.

(St. John Chrysostom, Homily 19 on Ephesians)

20

20

20

October 1

L et us increase our thanksgiving—not in words, nor in tongue, but in deeds and works, in mind and in heart. Let us give thanks unto Him with all our souls.

(St. John Chrysostom, Homily 19 on Ephesians)

20 ___

20 ___

20 ___

October 2

You are the comforter. You are the love that watches over and heals us. To You we sing the song: Alleluia!

(Akathist of Thanksgiving, Kontakion 8)

20 _____

20 _____

20 _____

October 3

The wise man knows how to give thanks also to God in all things, he considers the present life as nothing; therefore he is neither delighted with prosperity, nor grieved with the opposite condition.

(St. John Chrysostom, Homily 9 on Colossians)

20

20

20

October 4

The earth is full of the Lord's mercy.
By the word of the Lord the heavens were established,
And all the host of them by the breath of His mouth,
Who gathers the waters of the sea together as in a wineskin,
Who put the abysses in storehouses.

(PSALM 32:5–7)

20

20

20

October 5

Let us never fail to give God thanks continually for all these things, not only that He has freed us from these calamities, but that He also permitted them to happen; and let us acknowledge His abundant goodness!

(St. John Chrysostom, Homily 21 on the Statutes)

20

20

20

October 6

Let all the earth fear the Lord,
And let all the world's inhabitants be shaken by Him;
For He spoke, and they were made;
He commanded, and they were created.

(Psalm 32:8, 9)

20

20

20

October 7

Glory to You who spread out heaven and earth before me as pages in the book of eternal wisdom.

(Akathist of Thanksgiving, Ikos 1)

20

20

20

October 8

There are many who say, "Who will show us good things?" O Lord, the light of Your face was stamped upon us. You put gladness in my heart.

(Psalm 4:7, 8)

20 _____

20 _____

20 _____

October 9

Let not the brightness of human success fill your soul with immoderate joy; let not grief bring low your soul's high and lofty exaltation through sadness and anguish.

(ST. BASIL THE GREAT, HOMILY IV, *ON THE GIVING OF THANKS*)

20

20

20

October 10

My soul shall be praised in the Lord;
Let the gentle hear, and be glad.

(Psalm 33:3)

20___

20___

20___

October 11

Are we in poverty? Let us give thanks. Are we in sickness? Let us give thanks. Are we falsely accused? Let us give thanks: when we suffer affliction, let us give thanks.

(St. John Chrysostom, Homily 33 on Hebrews)

20

20

20

October 12

You shake the earth like a garment; You stack the waves of the sea up to the heavens.

(Akathist of Thanksgiving, Kontakion 6)

20

20

20

October 13

If I said, "My foot slipped,"
Your mercy, O Lord, helped me.
O Lord, according to the abundance of grief in my heart,
Your encouragements consoled my soul.

(Psalm 93:18,19)

20 _____

20 _____

20 _____

October 14

We should understand that amidst the trials of this life we must ask for the power of endurance rather than the glory, because the joyousness of reigning cannot precede the times of suffering.

(St. Leo the Great, Sermon 51, *On the Transfiguration*)

20

20

20

October 15

When I called upon You consciously for the first time in childhood, You heard my prayer, and filled my heart with the blessing of peace.

(Akathist of Thanksgiving, Ikos 8)

20

20

20

October 16

O All-Transcendent God (and what other name could describe You?), . . . You alone are beyond the power of speech, yet all that we speak stems from You.

(St. Gregory the Theologian, A Prayer to the All-Transcendent God)

| 20 |

| 20 |

| 20 |

OCTOBER 17

You I invoke, O God... who strips us of that which is not, and arrays us in that which is. God, who makes us worthy to be heard. God, who fortifies us.

(St. Augustine, *Soliloquies*)

20

20

20

October 18

If you are looking for everything in this world, what need is there for hope? What is hope? It is feeling confidence in things to come.

(St. John Chrysostom, Homily 14 on Romans)

| 20 |

| 20 |

| 20 |

October 19

Glory to You who ceaselessly watch over me; glory to You for the encounters You ordain for me.

(Akathist of Thanksgiving, Ikos 5)

20

20

20

October 20

Hail! O Christ, the Word and Wisdom and Power of God! What can we helpless ones give You in return for all Your good gifts? For all are Yours, and You ask naught from us save our salvation, You who Yourself are the Giver of this, and yet are grateful to those who receive it, through Your unspeakable goodness.

(St. John of Damascus, *An Exposition of the Orthodox Faith*)

20

20

20

October 21

I will bless the Lord at all times;
His praise shall continually be in my mouth.

(Psalm 33:2)

20

20

20

October 22

Glory to You who satisfy my desires with good things; glory to You who watch over me day and night.

(Akathist of Thanksgiving, Ikos 8)

20

20

20

October 23

Let us be trustful and in all things which befall us let us rejoice and give thanks to the merciful God, that we may pass through this present life with serenity.

(St. John Chrysostom, *Homily on the Paralytic Let Down through the Roof*)

20

20

20

October 24

When the sun is setting, when quietness falls like the peace of eternal sleep, and the silence of the spent day reigns, then in the splendor of its declining rays, filtering through the clouds, I see Your dwelling-place.

(Akathist of Thanksgiving, Ikos 4)

20

20

20

October 25

Almighty and merciful God, I most humbly and heartily thank Your divine majesty for Your lovingkindness and tender mercy, for You have heard my humble prayer and graciously granted me deliverance from my trouble and misery.

(A Prayer of Thanksgiving after Deliverance from Trouble)

20

20

20

October 26

Glory to You who cure sorrow and emptiness with the healing flow of time.

(Akathist of Thanksgiving, Ikos 8)

20

20

20

October 27

How is it that so many good things could arise of themselves? The daily light? The beautiful order and the forethought that exist in all things? The mazy dances of the stars? The equable course of nights and days? The regular gradation of nature in vegetables, and animals, and men? Who, tell me, is it that orders these?

(ST. JOHN CHRYSOSTOM, HOMILY 19 ON EPHESIANS)

20

20

20

October 28

Do not set your heart on your possessions,
And do not say, "I am independent."

(Wisdom of Sirach 5:1)

20

20

20

October 29

I give thanks to You, Lord of heaven and earth, giving praise to You for my first being and infancy, of which I have no memory.
(St. Augustine, *Confessions* I)

20

20

20

October 30

After Your blinding light, how drab, how colorless, how illusory all else seems. My soul clings to You.

(Akathist of Thanksgiving, Ikos 6)

20

20

20

October 31

We ought therefore everywhere to yield to Him and always to give thanks, and to bear all things contentedly, whether He bestows benefits or chastisement upon us, for this also is a species of benefit.

(St. John Chrysostom, *Homily on the Paralytic Let down through the Roof*)

20

20

20

November 1

A hard heart will suffer ruin in the end. . . .
A hard heart will be weighed down with pains.

(Wisdom of Sirach 3:24, 25)

20____

20____

20____

November 2

The labors of the field come as no suprise to tillers of the land; sailors are not astonished if they meet a storm at sea; sweats in the summer heat are the common experience of the hired hand; and to them that have chosen to live a holy life the afflictions of this present world cannot come unforeseen.

(St. Basil the Great, Letter 18)

20

20

20

November 3

Glory to You, beyond the boundaries of our aspirations.

(Akathist of Thanksgiving, Ikos 6)

20

20

20

November 4

I sought the Lord, and He heard me;
And He delivered me from all my sojourning.

(Psalm 33:5)

20

20

20

November 5

Let us always give thanks to God who loves man; not merely for our deliverance from fearful evils, but for their being permitted to overtake us — learning this from the divine Scriptures, as well as from the late events that have befallen us, that He ever disposes all things for our advantage, with that lovingkindness which is His attribute, which God grant, that we may continually enjoy, and so may obtain the kingdom of heaven.

(St. John Chrysostom, Homily 21 on the Statutes)

20

20

20

November 6

Oh, taste and see that the Lord is good;
Blessed is the man who hopes in Him.

(Psalm 33:9)

20

20

20

November 7

Glory to You for Your eternity in the midst of this passing world; glory to You for Your blessings, seen and unseen.

(Akathist of Thanksgiving, Ikos 1)

20

20

20

November 8

For at no time should a man freely praise God more than when he has passed through afflictions; nor, again, should he at any time give thanks more than when he finds rest from toil and temptations.

(St. Athanasius, Letter 10)

20

20

20

November 9

For let this be your work: to give thanks in your prayers both for the seen and the unseen, and for His benefits to the willing and unwilling, and for the kingdom, and for hell, and for tribulation, and for refreshment. For thus is the custom of the saints to pray, and to give thanks for the common benefits of all.

(St. John Chrysostom, Homily 10 on Colossians)

20

20

20

November 10

There is nothing that can take the place of a faithful friend,
And there is no way to measure his worth.
(Wisdom of Sirach 6:15)

20

20

20

November 11

You must be trained in the lessons of this life before you can live the calm and quiet life to come. You will achieve this without difficulty if you keep ever with you the charge to rejoice at all times.

(St. Basil the Great, Homily IV, *On the Giving of Thanks*)

20

20

20

November 12

As then God crowns us who undergo labors, and hardness, and countless toils, so does He crown those who hope. For the name of patience belongs to hard work and much endurance. Yet even this He has granted to the man that hopes, that He might solace the wearied soul.

(St. John Chrysostom, Homily 14 on Romans)

November 13

Glory to You for the love of parents, for the faithfulness of friends.

(Akathist of Thanksgiving, Ikos 5)

20

20

20

November 14

I will give thanks to You,
For I am fearfully and wondrously made;
Marvelous are Your works,
And my soul knows this very well.

(Psalm 138:14)

20

20

20

November 15

G lory to You who make immortal all that is lofty and good.

(Akathist of Thanksgiving, Ikos 8)

20

20

20

November 16

We who do not even know how to ask for what is fitting unless we have received of the Spirit, let us take care to offer up thanksgiving for all things, and let us bear all things nobly.

(St. John Chrysostom, Homily 33 on Hebrews)

20

20

20

November 17

Remember your Creator until the silver cord is removed,
And the golden flower is pressed together,
And the pitcher is shattered at the fountain,
And the wheel runs together at the well;
Then the dust returns to the earth as it was,
And the spirit returns to God who gave it.

(ECCLESIASTES 12:6, 7)

20

20

20

November 18

Where You are not, there is only emptiness; hearts are smitten with sadness; nature, and life itself, become sorrowful; where You are, the soul is filled with abundance, and its song resounds like a torrent of life: Alleluia!

(Akathist of Thanksgiving, Kontakion 4)

20

20

20

November 19

Man's duty, then, is obedience to God, who has proclaimed salvation manifold by the commandments. And confession is thanksgiving.

(St. Clement of Alexandria, *The Stromata*, Book VII)

20

20

20

November 20

Glory to You who promise us the longed-for meeting with our loved ones who have died.

(Akathist of Thanksgiving, Ikos 8)

20

20

20

November 21

How great are You in Your creation! How great are You in man.
(Akathist of Thanksgiving, Ikos 7)

20

20

20

November 22

Thank You, O Lord, for Your strength and guidance in my work. You are the fulfillment of all good things.

(A Prayer after Work)

20

20

20

November 23

It is fitting that we render thanks not only when rich, but also when poor, not when in health only, but also when sick, not when we thrive only, but also when we have to bear the reverse. For when our affairs are borne onward with a fair wind, to be thankful is not a matter of wonder. But when no small tempests be upon us, and the vessel veers about and is in jeopardy, then is the great time for displaying patience and goodness of heart.

(St. John Chrysostom, Homily 2 on Romans)

20

20

20

November 24

G lory to You who transfigure our lives with acts of kindness.
(Akathist of Thanksgiving, Ikos 9)

20

20

20

November 25

Would you rather appear more attractive? Be content with the Creator's fashioning. Why do you wear these bits of gold, as if to correct God's creation? Clothe yourself in alms; clothe yourself in benevolence; clothe yourself in modesty, humbleness. These make even the beautiful more becoming; these make even the ill formed to be well formed.

(St. John Chrysostom, Homily 10 on Colossians)

20

20

20

November 26

Glory to You for our unquenchable thirst for communion with God.

(Akathist of Thanksgiving, Ikos 6)

20

20

20

November 27

To not give God thanks in all things is to blame Him in some degree. It is man's folly to dare to murmur often against his Creator, not only in time of want, but also in time of plenty, so that, when something is not supplied, he complains, and when certain things are in abundance he is ungrateful.

(St. Leo the Great, Sermon 12)

20

20

20

November 28

Glory to You, who have made wonderfully sweet the keeping of Your commandments.

(Akathist of Thanksgiving, Ikos 9)

20

20

20

November 29

To You, O Lord, most excellent and most good, You Architect and Governor of the universe, thanks had been due unto You, our God, even had You willed that I should not survive my boyhood. For I existed even then; I lived, and felt, and was solicitous about my own well-being—a trace of that most mysterious unity from whence I had my being.

(St. Augustine, *Confessions* I)

20

20

20

November 30

Glory to You for the humbleness of the animals that serve me.
(Akathist of Thanksgiving, Ikos 5)

20 ___

20 ___

20 ___

December 1

Glory to You, who kindle within us dissatisfaction with earthly things.

(Akathist of Thanksgiving, Ikos 3)

20___

20___

20___

December 2

Let that which pleases God, please us too. Let us rejoice in whatever measure of gifts He gives. Let him who has used great possessions well, use small ones also well. Plenty and scarcity may be equally for our good, and even in spiritual progress we shall not be cast down at the smallness of the results, if our minds become not dry and barren.

(St. Leo the Great, Sermon 12)

20

20

20

December 3

Glory to You, who make Yourself known where man shows mercy to his neighbor.

(Akathist of Thanksgiving, Ikos 9)

20

20

20

December 4

B ring my soul out of prison
To give thanks to Your name, O Lord.

(Psalm 141:8)

20

20

20

December 5

Glory to You, who sends failure and misfortune to us that we may share in the sorrows of others.

(Akathist of Thanksgiving, Ikos 9)

20 _____

20 _____

20 _____

December 6

Dismiss the worries of the flesh. Gather together the joys of the soul. Rise above the sensible perception of present things. Fix your mind on the hope of things eternal. Of these the mere thought suffices to fill the soul with gladness, and to plant in our hearts the happiness of angels.

(St. Basil the Great, Homily IV, *On the Giving of Thanks*)

20

20

20

December 7

Glory to You through every sigh of my sadness, for every step of my life's journey, for every moment of happiness.

(Akathist of Thanksgiving, Ikos 1)

20

20

20

December 8

Love your soul and comfort your heart,
And put sorrow far away from you;
For sorrow has destroyed many,
And there is no profit in it.

(Wisdom of Sirach 30:23)

20

20

20

December 9

Glory to You, for all Nature is filled with Your power.
(Akathist of Thanksgiving, Ikos 7)

20

20

20

December 10

If a man lives many years
And rejoices in them all,
Yet let him remember the days of darkness,
For they shall be many.
All that comes is vanity.

(ECCLESIASTES 11:8)

20___

20___

20___

December 11

Glory to You for the love which You have raised above everything in heaven and on earth.

(Akathist of Thanksgiving, Ikos 9)

20

20

20

December 12

You who fear the Lord, hope for good things,
And for everlasting gladness and mercy.

(Wisdom of Sirach 2:9)

20

20

20

December 13

Glory to You who turn on us Your healing rays.
(Akathist of Thanksgiving, Ikos 6)

20____

20____

20____

December 14

Let us bear all things thankfully, be it poverty, be it disease, be it anything else whatever: for He alone knows the things expedient for us.

(St. John Chrysostom, Homily 33 on Hebrews)

20

20

20

December 15

Glory to You who welcome our moments of soaring.

(Akathist of Thanksgiving, Ikos 9)

20

20

20

December 16

Do you eat? Give thanks to God both before and afterwards. Do you sleep? Give thanks to God both before and afterwards. . . . Do all in the Name of the Lord, and all shall be prospered to you.

(St. John Chrysostom, Homily 9 on Colossians)

20

20

20

December 17

To speak with You is more soothing than anointing with oil, sweeter than the honeycomb. To pray to You lifts the spirit, refreshes the soul.

(Akathist of Thanksgiving, Kontakion 4)

20

20

20

December 18

B lessed is God, who is merciful to us and feeds us with His bountiful gifts by His divine grace.

(A Prayer after the Evening Meal)

20

20

20

December 19

Glory to You for Your goodness even in times of darkness when all the world is hidden from our eyes.

(Akathist of Thanksgiving, Ikos 4)

20

20

20

December 20

Be not dismayed or troubled but continue to give thanks to God for all things, praising and invoking Him; beseeching and supplicating; even if countless tumults and troubles come upon you, even if tempests are stirred up before your eyes, let none of these things disturb you. For our Master is not baffled by the difficulty, even if all things are reduced to the extremity of ruin.

(St. John Chrysostom, Letters to Olympias)

20

20

20

December 21

Your way is in the sea,
And Your paths are in many waters;
And Your footsteps shall not be known.

(Psalm 76:20)

20

20

20

December 22

For what you have received give thanks; and do not be angry on account of those things which you have not received. And, for what you know, give glory, and do not stumble at those things of which you are ignorant. For God has made both alike profitably; and has revealed some things, but hidden others, providing for your safety.

(St. John Chrysostom, Homily 12 on the Statutes)

20

20

20

December 23

I have loved, because the Lord
Shall hear the voice of my supplication.

(Psalm 114:1)

20

20

20

December 24

Let each one of us then be a dwelling-place for Him who loves us. Let us come to Him and make our abode with Him. This is the Godhead who though all creation cannot contain, yet a lowly and humble soul suffices to receive Him.

(St. Ephraim, *Homily on the Nativity of Our Lord*)

2 0

2 0

2 0

December 25

Though all the divine utterances exhort us, dearly beloved, to "rejoice in the Lord always" (Philippians 4:4), today we are incited to a full spiritual joy, as the mystery of the Lord's Nativity is shining brightly upon us.

(St. Leo the Great, Sermon 28)

20

20

20

December 26

N o one can put together what has crumbled into dust, but You can restore a conscience turned to ashes.

(Akathist of Thanksgiving, Kontakion 10)

20

20

20

December 27

Glory to You for every happening, every condition in which Your providence has put me.

(Akathist of Thanksgiving, Ikos 10)

20

20

20

December 28

We were filled with Your mercy in the morning,
And in all our days we greatly rejoiced and were glad;
Gladden us in return for the days You humbled us,
For the years we saw evil things.

(Psalm 89:14, 15)

20

20

20

December 29

Let the Christian always be grateful, never ungrateful: let him be grateful to his Father, who soothes and caresses him, and grateful to his Father when He chastens him with the scourge, and teaches him: for He ever loves, whether He caress or threaten. Let him say what you have heard in the Psalm: "It is a good thing to give thanks unto the Lord; and to sing praises unto Your Name, O Most High" (Psalm 91:1). (ST. AUGUSTINE, *Exposition on Psalm 92*)

20

20

20

December 30

Glory to You for the unforgettable moments of life; glory to You for the heart's innocent joy.

(Akathist of Thanksgiving, Ikos 5)

20

20

20

December 31

In all works of godliness let us use what each year gives us, and let not seasons of difficulty hinder our Christian benevolence. The Lord knows how to replenish the widow's vessels, which her pious deed of hospitality has emptied, He knows how to turn water into wine, He knows how to satisfy five thousand hungry persons with a few loaves.

(St. Leo the Great, Sermon 12)

20

20

20

33 Thanksgiving Prompts

1. What are five hobbies or activities that bring you joy?
2. What is one good thing that came out of the hardest situation you've ever faced?
3. What teacher or mentor has had a positive influence on your life? What are three qualities you admire about that person?
4. What is the tradition or ritual in your life you are most thankful for?
5. What was a time in your life when you had to wait for something, and what fruits did the season of waiting bring about?
6. What is your favorite location in your town or city and why?
7. What is one of the biggest lessons you learned in your childhood?
8. When was the last time you were surprised or encouraged by someone's thoughtfulness?
9. What is a recent setback you encountered, and what did you learn from it?
10. What is the funniest thing that happened today?
11. Who is one person who makes your life better and why?
12. Who is a difficult person in your life, and what qualities about them do you appreciate?
13. What is one positive thing you could say about today's weather?
14. What are seven things in your life you take for granted?
15. What physical sense are you most grateful for and why?
16. What is the most difficult thing you learned today?
17. What is one of your weaknesses, and how has being aware of it improved your outlook?
18. What are three things you can give thanks for now that you wouldn't have been able to ten years ago?

19. How were you able to make a difference today, however small?
20. What aspect(s) of your job or daily life do you most appreciate and why?
21. What is one thing you appreciated about today?
22. What is one of your favorite quotes?
23. What is an activity you don't enjoy but are usually glad when you do it? Why?
24. What is your favorite aspect of the current season and why?
25. What freedom(s) in your life are you most grateful for and why?
26. What fear is most dominating you right now, and what can you learn from it?
27. What are ten things in the room you are sitting in that you are thankful for?
28. When was a time you felt courageous? What made you feel brave?
29. What is your favorite childhood memory?
30. Who in your life has taught you the most about unconditional love?
31. When was a time you shifted your perspective in a meaningful way?
32. What made you laugh today?
33. Who helped you today?

About the Author

Dr. Nicole Roccas has a PhD in History from the University of Cincinnati and, in addition to being a writer and podcaster, she is an adjunct faculty member at the Orthodox School of Theology at Trinity College (Toronto). She is best known for her Ancient Faith Radio podcast *Time Eternal*. Her previous books are *Time and Despondency: Regaining the Present in Faith and Life* (Ancient Faith Publishing, 2017) and *Under the Laurel Tree: Grieving Infertility with Saints Joachim and Anna* (Ancient Faith Publishing, 2019). A native of Wisconsin, Nicole lives in Toronto with her husband, Basil, whose efforts to indoctrinate her into the ways of maple syrup and Canadian spelling are slowly paying off. Find more at her website: www.nicoleroccas.com

Ancient Faith Publishing hopes you have enjoyed and benefited from this book. The proceeds from the sales of our books only partially cover the costs of operating our nonprofit ministry—which includes both the work of **Ancient Faith Publishing** and the work of **Ancient Faith Radio**. Your financial support makes it possible to continue this ministry both in print and online. Donations are tax-deductible and can be made at **www.ancientfaith.com**.

To view our other publications,
please visit our website: **store.ancientfaith.com**

 ANCIENT FAITH RADIO

Bringing you Orthodox Christian music, readings,
prayers, teaching, and podcasts 24 hours a day since 2004 at
www.ancientfaith.com